EMMANUEL JOSEPH

Temporal Threads, Weaving History, Philosophy, and the Future of Technology

Copyright © 2025 by Emmanuel Joseph

All rights reserved. No part of this publication may be reproduced, stored or transmitted in any form or by any means, electronic, mechanical, photocopying, recording, scanning, or otherwise without written permission from the publisher. It is illegal to copy this book, post it to a website, or distribute it by any other means without permission.

First edition

This book was professionally typeset on Reedsy.
Find out more at reedsy.com

Contents

1. Chapter 1: The Loom of Time — 1
2. Chapter 2: Ancient Wisdom and Technological Marvels — 3
3. Chapter 3: The Renaissance Rebirth — 5
4. Chapter 4: The Enlightenment and the Age of Reason — 7
5. Chapter 5: The Industrial Revolution and Beyond — 9
6. Chapter 6: The Digital Age — 11
7. Chapter 7: The Age of Artificial Intelligence — 13
8. Chapter 8: The Interconnected World — 15
9. Chapter 9: Ethics in the Technological Era — 17
10. Chapter 10: The Human-Machine Interface — 19
11. Chapter 11: The Future of Work — 21
12. Chapter 12: The Role of Education — 23
13. Chapter 13: The Environmental Impact of Technology — 25
14. Chapter 14: The Ethics of Innovation — 27
15. Chapter 15: Weaving the Future — 29

1

Chapter 1: The Loom of Time

In the vast expanse of human history, the loom of time weaves intricate patterns, each thread representing an era or civilization. These threads intertwine, forming the fabric of our collective memory, a tapestry that tells the story of our existence. From the dawn of civilization to the present day, time has been both a silent witness and an active participant in shaping our destiny. It is through this lens that we can begin to understand the profound connections between history, philosophy, and technology.

Philosophers have long pondered the nature of time, exploring its elusive qualities and its impact on human consciousness. Ancient Greek philosophers like Heraclitus and Parmenides offered contrasting views on the fluidity and permanence of time, setting the stage for centuries of debate. The cyclical view of time in Eastern philosophies, such as Hinduism and Buddhism, presents a different perspective, where time is seen as an eternal cycle of creation and destruction.

As we delve deeper into history, we witness the pivotal moments that have defined the course of humanity. The invention of writing systems allowed for the preservation of knowledge, enabling future generations to build upon the wisdom of their predecessors. The Renaissance era, with its revival of classical knowledge and emphasis on human potential, marked a significant turning point in the trajectory of human progress. The Industrial Revolution, fueled by technological advancements, propelled society into an era of unprecedented change and innovation.

The future of technology holds the promise of even greater transformations, as we stand on the brink of the Fourth Industrial Revolution. This new era is characterized by the fusion of physical, digital, and biological worlds, blurring the boundaries between humans and machines. As we navigate this uncharted territory, it is essential to draw upon the lessons of history and philosophy to ensure that technological advancements align with our collective values and aspirations.

2

Chapter 2: Ancient Wisdom and Technological Marvels

The ancient world was a cradle of innovation, where the seeds of modern technology were sown. Civilizations such as Mesopotamia, Egypt, and the Indus Valley developed remarkable technologies that laid the foundation for future advancements. The invention of the wheel, the construction of monumental structures like the pyramids, and the development of sophisticated irrigation systems were testaments to human ingenuity and resourcefulness.

In ancient Greece, the birthplace of Western philosophy, thinkers like Aristotle and Archimedes made significant contributions to the understanding of science and technology. Aristotle's works on natural philosophy provided a framework for studying the physical world, while Archimedes' inventions, such as the screw pump and compound pulleys, demonstrated the practical applications of scientific knowledge. These early advancements paved the way for the scientific revolution that would follow centuries later.

The intersection of history and philosophy is vividly illustrated in the achievements of the ancient Chinese civilization. The invention of paper, the compass, gunpowder, and printing had a profound impact on human society, transforming communication, navigation, and warfare. Confucianism and Taoism, the dominant philosophical traditions of the time, emphasized the importance of harmony, balance, and ethical conduct, guiding the development and use of technology.

The ancient wisdom of these civilizations continues to resonate in the modern world, reminding us of the enduring principles that underlie technological progress. As we confront the challenges of the 21st century, it is crucial to draw upon the insights of the past, integrating them with contemporary knowledge to create a harmonious and sustainable future. By weaving together the threads of history, philosophy, and technology, we can create a tapestry that reflects the richness and complexity of the human experience.

3

Chapter 3: The Renaissance Rebirth

The Renaissance era, spanning the 14th to the 17th centuries, was a period of profound intellectual and artistic revival. It was characterized by a renewed interest in classical knowledge and a burgeoning spirit of inquiry that transcended disciplinary boundaries. This cultural rebirth was fueled by the rediscovery of ancient Greek and Roman texts, which inspired a new generation of scholars, artists, and inventors to explore the frontiers of human potential.

The philosophical underpinnings of the Renaissance were deeply rooted in humanism, a movement that emphasized the inherent dignity and worth of the individual. Humanist thinkers like Petrarch, Erasmus, and Pico della Mirandola championed the idea that humans possess the capacity for self-improvement through education and the pursuit of knowledge. This philosophical outlook laid the groundwork for the scientific revolution, which would forever alter our understanding of the natural world.

Technological advancements during the Renaissance were driven by a spirit of experimentation and innovation. The invention of the printing press by Johannes Gutenberg in the mid-15th century revolutionized the dissemination of knowledge, making books more accessible and fostering the spread of new ideas. Leonardo da Vinci, the quintessential Renaissance man, epitomized the interdisciplinary nature of the era, making significant contributions to art, science, and engineering. His visionary designs for flying machines, submarines, and other inventions showcased the limitless potential of human creativity.

The Renaissance also witnessed remarkable achievements in art and architecture, as artists like Michelangelo, Raphael, and Brunelleschi pushed the boundaries of their craft. The use of perspective in painting, the construction of domes and cathedrals, and the creation of lifelike sculptures demonstrated the harmonious integration of artistic expression and scientific principles. This period of artistic and intellectual flourishing laid the foundation for the modern world, shaping our cultural, scientific, and technological landscape.

4

Chapter 4: The Enlightenment and the Age of Reason

The Enlightenment, also known as the Age of Reason, was an intellectual movement that emerged in the 17th and 18th centuries, advocating reason, individualism, and skepticism of traditional authority. Enlightenment thinkers, known as philosophes, sought to apply the principles of rational inquiry to all aspects of human life, from science and politics to ethics and religion. This era of intellectual ferment laid the groundwork for the modern scientific and technological advancements that would follow.

Central to the Enlightenment was the belief in the power of human reason to uncover the truths of the natural world. Figures like Isaac Newton and Galileo Galilei made groundbreaking contributions to the field of science, challenging long-held beliefs and paving the way for the development of modern physics and astronomy. Newton's laws of motion and universal gravitation provided a new framework for understanding the physical universe, while Galileo's observations of the heavens using a telescope revolutionized our perception of the cosmos.

The Enlightenment also saw significant advancements in political philosophy, as thinkers like John Locke, Jean-Jacques Rousseau, and Montesquieu explored the nature of government and the rights of individuals. Locke's theories on natural rights and the social contract influenced the development of democratic principles and the formation of modern constitutional governments. Rousseau's ideas on education and civic responsibility emphasized the importance of nurturing the moral and intellectual potential of individuals.

Technological innovations during the Enlightenment were driven by a desire to improve the human condition and harness the power of nature for the benefit of society. The Industrial Revolution, which began in the late 18th century, was a direct result of Enlightenment principles, as inventors and engineers sought to apply scientific knowledge to practical problems. The development of steam engines, mechanized textile production, and advances in metallurgy transformed the economic and social landscape, ushering in an era of unprecedented growth and change.

5

Chapter 5: The Industrial Revolution and Beyond

The Industrial Revolution, which began in the late 18th century and continued into the 19th century, marked a period of profound technological and social transformation. The advent of new manufacturing processes, powered by steam engines and mechanized machinery, revolutionized industries such as textiles, transportation, and metallurgy. This era of rapid industrialization had far-reaching implications for society, shaping the modern world in ways that continue to resonate today.

The philosophical underpinnings of the Industrial Revolution were deeply influenced by Enlightenment principles, particularly the belief in progress and the power of human ingenuity. Thinkers like Adam Smith and John Stuart Mill explored the relationship between industrialization and economic prosperity, advocating for free markets and the pursuit of individual self-interest. The rise of capitalism and the growth of urban centers were direct consequences of these philosophical and economic ideas.

Technological advancements during the Industrial Revolution were driven by a spirit of innovation and experimentation. The development of the steam engine by James Watt, the invention of the spinning jenny by James Hargreaves, and the construction of the first steam-powered locomotives by George Stephenson were just a few examples of the groundbreaking innovations that defined this era. These technological achievements not only transformed industries but also had a profound impact on the daily lives of individuals, changing the way people worked, lived, and traveled.

The Industrial Revolution also brought about significant social and environmental challenges, as rapid urbanization and industrialization led to overcrowded cities, poor working conditions, and environmental degradation. Philosophers and social reformers like Karl Marx and Friedrich Engels critiqued the excesses of capitalism and called for the establishment of more equitable and just societies. Their ideas laid the foundation for the development of socialist and communist movements, which sought to address the social injustices and inequalities brought about by industrialization.

6

Chapter 6: The Digital Age

The advent of the digital age in the late 20th and early 21st centuries has ushered in a new era of technological innovation and societal transformation. The rapid development and widespread adoption of digital technologies, such as the internet, personal computers, and smartphones, have fundamentally changed the way we communicate, work, and live. This digital revolution has created new opportunities for economic growth, social connectivity, and cultural exchange, while also presenting new challenges and ethical dilemmas.

The philosophical implications of the digital age are vast and multifaceted. The proliferation of information and the rise of social media have transformed the way we perceive and interact with the world, raising questions about privacy, identity, and the nature of reality. The digital age has also given rise to new ethical dilemmas, such as the impact of artificial intelligence on employment and the potential for technology to be used for surveillance and control.

Technological advancements in the digital age have been driven by the convergence of various fields, including computer science, telecommunications, and electronics. The development of the internet has revolutionized communication, enabling instant access to information and connecting people across the globe. The rise of social media platforms has created new opportunities for social interaction and cultural exchange, while also presenting challenges related to misinformation, privacy, and mental health.

The digital age has also witnessed the rise of new economic paradigms, as the advent of e-commerce and digital currencies has transformed the way we conduct business and manage financial transactions. The sharing economy, characterized by platforms like Uber and Airbnb, has disrupted traditional industries and created new opportunities for entrepreneurship and innovation. At the same time, these developments have raised important questions about labor rights, economic inequality, and the regulation of emerging technologies.

As we navigate the complexities of the digital age, it is essential to draw upon the insights of history and philosophy to guide our approach to technology. By reflecting on the lessons of the past and considering the ethical implications of technological advancements, we can work towards creating a future that is both innovative and inclusive. The digital age offers unparalleled opportunities for human progress, but it also requires careful consideration and responsible stewardship to ensure that its benefits are shared by all.

7

Chapter 7: The Age of Artificial Intelligence

Artificial intelligence (AI) represents one of the most significant technological advancements of the 21st century, with the potential to transform every aspect of human life. From healthcare and education to transportation and entertainment, AI is poised to revolutionize industries and create new possibilities for innovation and growth. However, the rise of AI also raises important ethical and philosophical questions about the nature of intelligence, agency, and the role of technology in society.

The development of AI has been driven by advances in machine learning, neural networks, and big data, enabling machines to perform tasks that were once thought to be the exclusive domain of humans. AI systems are now capable of recognizing patterns, making decisions, and even engaging in creative processes, such as generating art and composing music. These capabilities have the potential to enhance human productivity and creativity, but they also raise concerns about the displacement of jobs and the impact on human identity and autonomy.

Philosophers and ethicists have long debated the implications of artificial intelligence, exploring questions about the nature of consciousness, the ethics of machine decision-making, and the potential for AI to surpass human intelligence. The concept of the singularity, a hypothetical point at which

AI becomes self-aware and surpasses human intelligence, has been a topic of both fascination and concern. While some view the singularity as an opportunity for unprecedented progress, others caution against the potential risks and unintended consequences.

As we continue to develop and integrate AI into our lives, it is crucial to consider the ethical implications and ensure that AI is designed and used in ways that align with human values and priorities. This requires a multidisciplinary approach, drawing on insights from history, philosophy, and technology to create a framework for responsible AI development. By fostering a dialogue that includes diverse perspectives, we can work towards a future where AI enhances human well-being and promotes a more just and equitable society.

8

Chapter 8: The Interconnected World

The advent of the digital age has ushered in an era of unprecedented interconnectedness, where the boundaries between nations, cultures, and individuals are increasingly blurred. The rapid development of communication technologies, such as the internet and social media, has created a global village, enabling people to connect, share ideas, and collaborate across vast distances. This interconnected world offers new opportunities for cultural exchange, economic growth, and social progress, while also presenting challenges related to governance, privacy, and security.

The philosophical implications of a connected world are profound, as they raise questions about identity, community, and the nature of human relationships. The ability to connect with others across the globe has transformed the way we perceive ourselves and our place in the world, fostering a sense of global citizenship and interconnectedness. At the same time, the digital age has also given rise to new forms of social isolation and fragmentation, as individuals navigate the complexities of online interactions and digital communities.

Technological advancements in communication have been driven by innovations in computer science, telecommunications, and data analytics. The development of the World Wide Web, social media platforms, and mobile technologies has revolutionized the way we communicate, enabling instant access to information and real-time interactions. These technologies have created new opportunities for collaboration and innovation, while also raising important questions about the impact on privacy, security, and the dissemination of information.

As we navigate the challenges and opportunities of an interconnected world, it is essential to draw upon the insights of history and philosophy to guide our approach to technology and governance. By reflecting on the lessons of the past and considering the ethical implications of technological advancements, we can work towards creating a future that is both innovative and inclusive. The interconnected world offers unparalleled opportunities for human progress, but it also requires careful consideration and responsible stewardship to ensure that its benefits are shared by all.

9

Chapter 9: Ethics in the Technological Era

The rapid pace of technological advancement in the modern era has brought about profound changes in the way we live, work, and interact with the world. As we navigate these changes, it is essential to consider the ethical implications of our actions and the impact of technology on society. The field of ethics provides a framework for evaluating the moral dimensions of technological innovation, guiding our decisions and ensuring that technology serves the greater good.

Philosophers and ethicists have long grappled with the challenges posed by technological progress, exploring questions about the nature of morality, the responsibilities of individuals and institutions, and the principles that should guide our actions. The development of artificial intelligence, biotechnology, and digital technologies has raised new ethical dilemmas, such as the implications of genetic engineering, the impact of AI on employment, and the role of technology in shaping human behavior.

One of the central ethical challenges of the technological era is the question of privacy and data security. The widespread collection and analysis of personal data by governments, corporations, and other entities have raised concerns about the erosion of privacy and the potential for abuse. Ethical considerations must guide the development and implementation of technologies to ensure that individual rights and freedoms are protected.

Another important ethical issue is the impact of technology on social and economic inequality. Technological advancements have the potential to create new opportunities for economic growth and social progress, but they can also exacerbate existing disparities. It is essential to consider the distributional effects of technology and to develop policies that promote inclusivity and equity.

As we continue to develop and integrate new technologies into our lives, it is crucial to engage in an ongoing ethical dialogue, drawing on the insights of history, philosophy, and technology. By fostering a multidisciplinary approach and considering diverse perspectives, we can work towards creating a future where technology enhances human well-being and promotes a more just and equitable society.

10

Chapter 10: The Human-Machine Interface

The integration of technology into every aspect of human life has transformed the way we interact with the world and with each other. The human-machine interface, the point of interaction between humans and technology, is a critical area of study that explores the design, usability, and impact of technological systems. From personal computers and smartphones to virtual reality and wearable devices, the human-machine interface shapes our experiences and influences our behavior.

Philosophers and technologists have long been interested in the relationship between humans and machines, exploring questions about the nature of human cognition, the potential for augmentation, and the ethical implications of technological integration. The development of user-centered design principles and human-computer interaction (HCI) methodologies has sought to create technologies that are intuitive, accessible, and responsive to human needs.

One of the most significant advancements in the human-machine interface is the development of virtual and augmented reality technologies. These immersive experiences have the potential to transform education, entertainment, healthcare, and other fields by providing new ways of interacting with information and environments. The ethical implications of these technologies, such as the potential for addiction, the impact on mental health, and the blurring of the boundaries between reality and virtuality, must be carefully considered.

Another important area of study is the development of wearable technologies, such as smartwatches, fitness trackers, and implantable devices. These technologies have the potential to enhance human capabilities and provide valuable health and wellness information, but they also raise questions about privacy, consent, and the long-term effects of technological integration.

As we continue to explore the human-machine interface, it is essential to draw on the insights of history, philosophy, and technology to guide our approach. By considering the ethical implications and focusing on the needs and experiences of users, we can create technologies that enhance human well-being and promote a more harmonious relationship between humans and machines.

11

Chapter 11: The Future of Work

The rapid pace of technological advancement in the modern era is transforming the nature of work and the workplace. Automation, artificial intelligence, and digital technologies are reshaping industries, creating new opportunities and challenges for workers, employers, and policymakers. The future of work is a critical area of study that explores the impact of technology on employment, productivity, and economic growth, as well as the ethical and social implications of these changes.

Philosophers and economists have long been interested in the relationship between technology and work, exploring questions about the nature of labor, the value of work, and the impact of technological progress on economic and social systems. The development of automation and AI has raised concerns about the displacement of jobs and the potential for increased economic inequality. At the same time, these technologies offer new opportunities for these technologies offer new opportunities for innovation, productivity, and economic growth.

One of the central questions in the future of work is the impact of automation and AI on employment. While some jobs may be displaced by machines, new opportunities will also emerge in fields such as AI development, data analysis, and cybersecurity. The challenge for policymakers and educators is to ensure that workers have the skills and training needed to adapt to these changes and thrive in the evolving job market. Lifelong learning and reskilling initiatives will be crucial in preparing the workforce for the demands of the future.

The gig economy, characterized by short-term contracts and freelance work, has also transformed the nature of employment. Platforms like Uber, TaskRabbit, and Upwork have created new opportunities for individuals to earn income and gain flexibility in their work schedules. However, the gig economy also raises important questions about job security, worker rights, and the social safety net. Ensuring that gig workers have access to benefits and protections will be an important consideration in the future of work.

The rise of remote work, accelerated by the COVID-19 pandemic, has also had a profound impact on the workplace. Advances in communication and collaboration technologies have enabled individuals to work from anywhere, creating new possibilities for work-life balance and reducing the need for physical office spaces. However, remote work also presents challenges related to team cohesion, productivity, and the blurring of boundaries between work and personal life.

As we navigate the future of work, it is essential to draw on the insights of history, philosophy, and technology to guide our approach. By considering the ethical implications and focusing on the needs and well-being of workers, we can create a future where technology enhances human productivity and promotes a more equitable and inclusive economy.

12

Chapter 12: The Role of Education

Education is a cornerstone of human development and progress, providing individuals with the knowledge, skills, and values needed to navigate the complexities of the modern world. The rapid pace of technological advancement in the 21st century has transformed the landscape of education, creating new opportunities and challenges for learners, educators, and institutions. The role of education in the digital age is a critical area of study that explores the impact of technology on teaching and learning, as well as the ethical and social implications of these changes.

Philosophers and educators have long been interested in the nature and purpose of education, exploring questions about the development of human potential, the cultivation of virtue, and the preparation for civic life. The rise of digital technologies has raised new questions about the role of education in a rapidly changing world, such as the need for digital literacy, the impact of online learning, and the potential for technology to enhance or detract from the educational experience.

One of the most significant advancements in education is the development of online learning platforms, such as MOOCs (massive open online courses) and virtual classrooms. These technologies have the potential to democratize education by providing access to high-quality learning resources for individuals around the world. However, online learning also presents challenges related to engagement, equity, and the digital divide. Ensuring that all learners have access to the technology and support needed to succeed in the digital age is a critical consideration.

The integration of AI and personalized learning technologies into education has also created new possibilities for individualized instruction and support. AI-powered tutoring systems, adaptive learning platforms, and data analytics can provide insights into student performance and tailor instruction to meet the needs of each learner. However, the use of AI in education also raises ethical questions about data privacy, algorithmic bias, and the potential for surveillance.

As we explore the role of education in the digital age, it is essential to draw on the insights of history, philosophy, and technology to guide our approach. By considering the ethical implications and focusing on the needs and well-being of learners, we can create an educational system that prepares individuals for the challenges and opportunities of the future.

13

Chapter 13: The Environmental Impact of Technology

The rapid pace of technological advancement in the modern era has had a profound impact on the natural environment, creating both opportunities and challenges for sustainability. The relationship between technology and the environment is a critical area of study that explores the impact of technological innovation on ecological systems, the potential for technology to address environmental challenges, and the ethical implications of our actions.

Philosophers and environmentalists have long been interested in the relationship between humans and the natural world, exploring questions about the value of nature, the responsibilities of individuals and societies, and the principles that should guide our actions. The development of industrial technologies and the rise of consumer culture have raised new ethical dilemmas, such as the impact of pollution, climate change, and resource depletion.

One of the most significant environmental challenges of the 21st century is climate change, driven by the accumulation of greenhouse gases in the atmosphere. Technological innovations, such as renewable energy, electric vehicles, and carbon capture and storage, have the potential to mitigate the impact of climate change and transition to a more sustainable energy system.

However, the deployment of these technologies also raises questions about the social and economic implications, such as the impact on jobs, communities, and global equity.

The development of sustainable technologies, such as green building materials, circular economy practices, and precision agriculture, also offers new opportunities for reducing the environmental impact of human activities. These innovations have the potential to create more efficient and resilient systems, but they also require careful consideration of the ethical and social implications.

As we navigate the environmental impact of technology, it is essential to draw on the insights of history, philosophy, and technology to guide our approach. By considering the ethical implications and focusing on the needs and well-being of both humans and the natural world, we can create a future where technology enhances sustainability and promotes a more harmonious relationship with the environment.

14

Chapter 14: The Ethics of Innovation

Innovation is a driving force behind human progress, creating new possibilities for economic growth, social development, and technological advancement. However, the rapid pace of innovation also raises important ethical questions about the impact of new technologies on individuals, societies, and the environment. The ethics of innovation is a critical area of study that explores the moral dimensions of technological progress, guiding our decisions and ensuring that innovation serves the greater good.

Philosophers and ethicists have long grappled with the challenges posed by innovation, exploring questions about the nature of progress, the responsibilities of individuals and institutions, and the principles that should guide our actions. The development of emerging technologies, such as AI, biotechnology, and nanotechnology, has raised new ethical dilemmas, such as the implications of genetic engineering, the potential for unintended consequences, and the role of technology in shaping human behavior.

One of the central ethical challenges of innovation is the question of risk and uncertainty. The rapid pace of technological change means that we often do not fully understand the potential consequences of new technologies. This requires a precautionary approach, balancing the potential benefits of innovation with the need to mitigate risks and protect against harm.

Another important ethical issue is the impact of innovation on social and economic inequality. Technological advancements have the potential to create new opportunities for economic growth and social progress, but they can also exacerbate existing disparities. It is essential to consider the distributional effects of innovation and to develop policies that promote inclusivity and equity.

As we continue to innovate and develop new technologies, it is crucial to engage in an ongoing ethical dialogue, drawing on the insights of history, philosophy, and technology. By fostering a multidisciplinary approach and considering diverse perspectives, we can work towards creating a future where innovation enhances human well-being and promotes a more just and equitable society.

15

Chapter 15: Weaving the Future

As we stand on the brink of a new era of technological innovation and societal transformation, it is essential to draw on the insights of history, philosophy, and technology to guide our approach. The threads of the past, present, and future are woven together to create the tapestry of human experience, reflecting the richness and complexity of our journey.

The future of technology holds the promise of unprecedented advancements in fields such as AI, biotechnology, and renewable energy, offering new possibilities for human progress and sustainability. However, these advancements also raise important ethical and philosophical questions about the nature of humanity, the responsibilities of individuals and societies, and the principles that should guide our actions.

By reflecting on the lessons of history and considering the ethical implications of technological progress, we can work towards creating a future that is both innovative and inclusive. This requires a multidisciplinary approach, drawing on the insights of philosophers, historians, technologists, and ethicists to navigate the complexities of the modern world.

As we weave the future, it is essential to focus on the needs and well-being of individuals and communities, ensuring that technological advancements align with our collective values and aspirations. By fostering a dialogue that includes diverse perspectives and promotes responsible stewardship, we can create a tapestry that reflects the best of human potential and enhances the quality of life for all.

The journey of "Temporal Threads" is a testament to the enduring connections between history, philosophy, and technology. As we continue to explore the intersections of these fields, we can weave a future that honors the past, embraces the present, and inspires the possibilities of tomorrow.

Temporal Threads: Weaving History, Philosophy, and the Future of Technology

In "Temporal Threads," journey through the intricate tapestry of human existence where history, philosophy, and technology intertwine. This book explores the profound connections between these fields, drawing upon the wisdom of ancient civilizations, the intellectual fervor of the Renaissance, and the groundbreaking advancements of the digital age. From the philosophical inquiries of Greek thinkers to the revolutionary ideas of the Enlightenment, and from the transformative power of the Industrial Revolution to the ethical dilemmas posed by artificial intelligence, "Temporal Threads" provides a comprehensive and thought-provoking exploration of our past, present, and future.

By reflecting on the lessons of history and considering the ethical implications of technological progress, "Temporal Threads" offers a roadmap for navigating the complexities of the modern world. This book invites readers to ponder the enduring principles that underlie technological advancement and to envision a future that is both innovative and inclusive. With its multidisciplinary approach, "Temporal Threads" weaves together the threads of history, philosophy, and technology to create a rich and compelling narrative that celebrates human potential and inspires the possibilities of tomorrow.

www.ingramcontent.com/pod-product-compliance
Lightning Source LLC
LaVergne TN
LVHW010443070526
838199LV00066B/6171